William Short

Christian science

William Short

Christian science

ISBN/EAN: 9783337263195

Printed in Europe, USA, Canada, Australia, Japan

Cover: Foto ©Lupo / pixelio.de

More available books at **www.hansebooks.com**

Christian Science

What it is, What is New, and What is True about it

BY

REV. WILLIAM SHORT, M. A.

RECTOR ST. PETER'S CHURCH, ST. LOUIS, MO.

WITH INTRODUCTION BY

Rt. Rev. HUGH MILLER THOMPSON, D.D., LL.D.

BISHOP OF MISSISSIPPI

NEW YORK
THOMAS WHITTAKER
2 AND 3 BIBLE HOUSE
1899

CONTENTS.

CHAPTER I.

A NEW RELIGION, AND SOME OF ITS CHARACTERISTICS.

PAGE

Various sects—Its origin—Souvenir spoons—The Gospel
of—Science and health—A rediscovery—The Key-
stone of the system—Claims prove nothing—An effort at self-deception—A bad form of bigotry—The
old path safer   1

CHAPTER II.

THE NAME A MISNOMER.

Neither Christian nor scientific—A bid for popularity—
Illogical conclusions—Cabalistic 20

CHAPTER III.

THE PHILOSOPHY OF CHRISTIAN SCIENCE DANGEROUS AND
IMMORAL.

An intellectual sin, and logical comedy—A formula for
immorality—Appeal to history—Its theology pantheistic 28

CHAPTER IV.

MENTAL HEALING EXPLAINED.

Methods of disarming criticism—A lost heritage—The
methods of Jesus—The principle the same—The
power of healing the birthright of man—Psychic
forces control functions—The secret revealed—The
two minds—Testimony of physicians—Shall the
Church endeavor to regain its lost heritage?—Conclusion 38

APPENDIX 57

Introduction.

THERE has been growing up of late, I am told, a thing calling itself *Christian Science.* Personally, I have not been brought into contact with it. Except by what I see in the ordinary printing in newspapers and the reading of books for or against it, I am uninformed about its present conditions. I identify it, however, without difficulty.

Its headquarters are, I am told, in Boston, and it has also representatives in Chicago and other towns.

It seems it has made considerable noise also in St. Louis.—So much noise that the Rev. William Short, the author of these lectures, felt it his duty to deliver them in his Church first, and then to reprint them.

I read the Lectures with great interest. It is but according to ancient wisdom to say, "There is nothing new under the sun," and it seems that the ancient Gnosticism of the earliest centuries, the "Anti-Christ that is even now come," is working again under the same

v

conditions. We have a *melange*, as of old, of
Oriental mysticism and thaumaturgy, under
Christian names, an attempt to connect our
Lord with the wild dreams of Eastern Pantheism, and to turn His religion, His morals
and ethics, into contempt, because the Body
which He wore, in which He was crucified,
which died and rose again, is only a dream, a
phantasm—may do what it will without sin,
because Sin, like the Body, has no existence!

It is interesting to note, as the philosophic
Historian will, that Gnosticism in the modern
form of Christian Science, Occultism, and other
degenerations of Human Intelligence, arises
and flourishes under the same conditions as it
did 1900 years ago.

A civilization, rich, luxurious, utterly material, a political corruption profound, and accepted, an absence of spiritual apprehension
in morals and ethics, great intelligence, and a
debased family life; a degeneration in manhood, and especially in the shameless and pitiful conditions among womankind—so that the
untranslatable epigrams of Martial can describe
life in New York, Chicago, or Boston as they
did in Rome in its rottenness—that conditions
like these should find expression in an utterly
sensual philosophy, under spiritual names, in
a caricature of Christianity which leaves out

duty, in principles which, logically followed, justify and lead to all uncleanness, does not surprise a philosopher.

In this Gnosticism, as old as Christianity, women have been especially prominent, from Helena, the mistress of Simon Magus down, sometimes as originators and leaders, mostly as the helpers and exhibitors for the men.

The author of these Lectures has brought out the real nature of this so-called "Christian Science" as another form of the old *Anti-Christianism*, which, known as Gnosticism, Manicheism, or what not, denies the existence of the Human Body, or blames the Body for all evil—and so, as he shows, has logically always led to the denial of bodily sin—for how can that which does not exist commit sin?

He is careful to say that those who are teaching this wild Hinduism (for it was from the first an attempt to graft Orientalism on Christianity) are not conscious of the outcome. They never were. They never reason to conclusions. Many of the originators, in the old days, were even stern ascetics.—Since the body has no existence, why shall I pay any heed to it?—but the *end* was always the same. "The Body is nothing, the material world is nothing. No other man's or woman's body has any real existence. The real Humanity cannot be affected by anything these non-existent bodies do with other non-existent bodies or things."

It turned out rather bad results in Alexandria, Corinth, Ephesus, and other highly civilized centres of wealth and culture. Will it be a gospel leading to high thoughts and lofty living in such unsensuous and spiritually-minded communities as Boston and Chicago?

It is well that the author, and other clergy are paying especial attention to the new form of the old Anti-Christianism. It is not mere silliness, nor a meaningless insanity.

HUGH MILLER THOMPSON.

BATTLE HILL, MISS., May 20, 1899.

"Beloved, believe not every Spirit, but try the Spirits whether they are of God; because many false prophets are gone out into the world.—1 JOHN iv. 1.

CHAPTER I.

THERE is a movement of thought and of
practical living which has attracted much
attention of late, which is popularly known as
Christian Science. Having started only about
thirty years ago, it now claims some 400
societies in the United States, which it calls
churches, and has some 5,000 teachers and
healers, who are said to be engaged in propa-
gating its peculiar tenets. By the force of its
new enthusiasm, the novelty of its methods
and the strangeness of its rather startling
doctrines, it has attracted widespread attention, and induced not a few to leave their own
churches to join it, as the newest religion of
Jesus Christ.

I speak of Christian Science as a new
religion, because while it is primarily a theory
of mental therapeutics, yet it claims to be
more. Its purpose is avowedly religious, and
its aim is nothing less than the reconstruction
of all human life, after theories and methods
which are peculiarly its own. It claims to

1

have a new gospel for mankind, and has organized societies to practice and to preach its precepts. It is so imbued with a sense of its own supreme sufficiency, as the only, and complete exponent of all divine truth, that it ignores all existing churches and organizes another sect—to add to the distraction of an already disorganized Christianity.

Now, if this movement was simply a new system of therapeutics, it would demand our calm and careful consideration on account of the remarkable cures that it assuredly does effect, but as it also calls itself Christian and claims to be based on the teaching and example of Jesus, it behooves us to examine into its credentials and to heed the admonition of St. John, who said: "Beloved, believe not every spirit, but try the spirits whether they are of God; because many false prophets have gone out into the world."

I desire, in these pages, to give you the result of my endeavor to "try the spirit" of Christian Science. And I wish to say that in my examination I have sought to be as fair and impartial as I could. I began my study of it in a sympathetic spirit, as a learner seeking after truth. Believing as I did, that no movement could take hold of so many intelligent minds with the power that Christian

Science has, unless there was some vital truth at the basis of it, I endeavored to approach the subject with an open mind, in order to ascertain what truth there was in it. Then, too, I felt that if Christian Science had any truth which Jesus taught as a part of his revelation to men, which the wants of a new age had called into prominence, that it was a part of the heritage of the Christian church, which she ought to embrace and utilize for the furtherance of Christ's purposes in the world. For I believe that the church of Jesus Christ ought to stand for all that is Christian. If there is any new revelation of the meaning and power of the truth which He taught, or any new manifestation of it, or any new emphasis of any old and neglected truth which can rightly claim the name of Christian, then I believe that the Christian church ought to be large enough and catholic enough and progressive enough to accept it and assimilate it, and turn its ethical forces into service for the blessing and salvation of mankind.

When I heard of people leaving their own churches to join Christian Scientists, it seemed to me that it surely ought not to be, that any earnest follower of Jesus should feel compelled to leave the church of Jesus Christ, in order to accept any truth which Jesus taught.

It was in this spirit that I began my study of this movement.

VARIOUS SECTS.

The first thing that confronts one, in studying what is known as Christian Science, is the fact, that the spirit of discord has already entered into its ranks, and divided the followers of Mrs. Eddy, into a number of opposing sects. Some of these manifest their religious zeal, by calling the others heretics, and disfellowship all who refuse to pronounce their own peculiar and distinctive shibboleths. As a sample of that "odium theologicum," which unfortunately seems quite natural to all religions, an article in a recent magazine,* gives an illustration. After speaking of the necessity for careful discrimination, the writer says "The name 'Christian Science' should be limited solely to the doctrines and methods and text-books and church of Mrs. Eddy, author of 'Science and Health,' with which half fanatical, personality-worshipping movement the New Thought has no more connection than exists between the Free Religious Association and the Pope of Rome." Those who represent the best thought and spirit of the movement, are beginning to disown and repudiate the name

* *Arena*, Feb., 1899.

of Christian Scientists, yet I shall use the term in a general and comprehensive sense, as that by which the movement is most familiarly known. It is unnecessary to enter into the differences, which divide its adherents into opposing schools of thought.

ITS ORIGIN.

To find out what Christian Science is, let us glance at its origin. Mrs. Mary Baker Glover Eddy, who claims to have been its founder, and who practically asserts her own infallibility, and is so regarded by some of the more ignorant of her followers, begins her book entitled " Science and Health" with this statement : " In the year 1866 I discovered the science of metaphysical healing, and named it Christian Science." Primarily, then it was a theory or system of mental therapeutics.*

* Christian Scientists object to having their religion referred to as *primarily a system of therapeutics*. But that this is true, in point of time, Mrs. Eddy herself states in the passage quoted. That it is also true, in point of fact, the whole underlying ground work of Science and Health shows. See especially chapter 12. Its therapeutics is not only the secret of the success of Christian Science, but it is the corner stone of the system. Christian Science lecturers, while they deny this, yet they continually refer to its cures, and speak of them as "demonstrations" of its truth. Its therapeutics was the central point, around which the whole system was constructed.

Mrs. Eddy states in her preface that "When God called her to proclaim His Gospel to this age, there came also the charge to plant and water His vineyard." So, in 1867, she opened a school of Christian Science mind healing, to instruct practitioners in her methods. Now the founder of Christian Science makes much of the principles and teaching of Jesus, but in carrying on this school for the prophets of the new faith she seems to have been actuated by something more mundane and mercenary than his example. For instance, the charge for the primary course in this school was 300 sordid and material dollars; for the normal course, $200; for the course in obstetrics, $100, and for the theological course, $200 more—altogether $800 in hard, material bank notes, exclusive of board, and strictly in advance. Now, inasmuch as such useless things as anatomy, physiology and materia medica were ignored in this school, the courses only occupied a few weeks and practitioners were turned out with remarkable rapidity. Mrs. Eddy states that during seven years she had some 4,000 students. Mrs. Eddy was also pastor of the first Christian Science church. In 1875 she issued the first edition of "Science and Health." The price for this book is three dollars, and, inasmuch as Mrs. Eddy is said to

be her own publisher, and the book has reached
its 163d edition, it is not to be wondered at that
the preface closes with this note: "The author
takes no patients, and declines medical consul-
tation."

SOUVENIR SPOONS.*

In addition to this, the founder of Christian
Science has recently launched forth in the
Souvenir Spoon business. The following is
from the *Christian Science Sentinel* of Jan.
26, 1899:

"On each of these most beautiful spoons is
a motto in bas-relief that every person on
earth needs to hold in thought. Mother
requests that Christian Scientists shall not
ask to be informed what this motto is, but
each Scientist shall purchase at least one
spoon, and those who can afford it, one dozen
spoons, that their families may read this
motto at every meal and their guests be made
partakers of its simple truth.

"MARY BAKER EDDY.

* The souvenir spoons which "Mother" Eddy urges, *as a
means of grace*, at three dollars each for plain silver, and five
dollars, gold-plated, contain a medallion of Mrs. Eddy on the
handle, an etching of Mrs. Eddy's home at Concord, N. H., in
the bowl, and on the back, a text from Mrs. Eddy's book, "Science and Health."

Now the ordinary "mortal mind" is quite justified in regarding this as a shrewd bit of business, under the garb of piety, and it does seem as if the dollars in it, stick out very large in "Mother" Eddy's spirituality. It is on a par with the doings of a certain Christian Science doctor, in Chicago, who is said to use his sermons as a part of his advertisements, with expressions on one page, such as— "Christ has come to his people," "He hath clothed his Church with the gifts of healing," "He hath anointed me to preach the Gospel to the poor"; and on a following page, "Terms will be forwarded on application," "Hot and cold water and porcelain baths in nearly all rooms," "All the comforts of a first-class hotel."

The commercial side to the early history of Christian Science is referred to, not only to show that its founder had what most people would call an "eye to business," in the method of her revelation of its blessings to mankind, but also because there are some who think that the same factor helps to explain the enthusiasm of some of its practitioners to-day. Yet it would be unfair to intimate that a mercenary spirit was prominent as a motive, with the great majority of its followers. Far from it, since there is no doubt that Christian Scientists,

as a rule, are as purely unselfish and self-sacri-
ficing people, as are found in any of our
churches.

THE GOSPEL OF CHRISTIAN SCIENCE.

The gospel of the orthodox Christian
Scientists is contained in the book referred to,
of some 600 pages, entitled "SCIENCE AND
HEALTH." If the author is correct, this the
"only true and authoritative exposition of the
science of metaphysical healing." "Those who
depart from this method forfeit their claims to
belong to its school." (Page 6.) *

The author implies that her system of
mind healing was a divine revelation,[1] and
says that while other methods "may have
occasional gleams of divinity," "yet they remain intensely human in their origin and
tendency, and are not scientifically Christian."
Yet the human in the author comes out quite
strong, only a few lines below, in her effort to
guard the rights and privileges (and per-
quisites) of her discovery. (Page 6.)

SCIENCE AND HEALTH.

The book, "Science and Health," is a most
remarkable production. In its entire disregard

* Page references are to *Science and Health*, 118th edition.
[1] See Note 1, Appendix. Mrs. Eddy's "Revelation."

of all common sense it leaves Jules Verne entirely in the rear. Now, I am aware, that those who accept its teachings will attribute any adverse criticism to prejudice or misunderstanding. Yet, after a second examination of it I can say without any exaggeration that from a literary standpoint it is simply beneath criticism. There are many good thoughts in it, and many practical and beautiful suggestions in it, but it is chiefly made up of the most astonishing propositions, strung together in the most inconsequential and disjointed way, without any logical sequence in the process of its thought, but iterated and reiterated in the most dogmatic manner, as if boldness of assumption was more convincing than reasonable argument. On page seven the author summarizes the fundamentals of Christian Science in the four following propositions:

" 1. God is all in all.

" 2. God is good. God is mind.

" 3. God, Spirit, being all, nothing is matter.

" 4. Life, God, omnipotent good, deny death, evil, sin, disease."

Then the author repeats the last proposition backward, and remarks that " the metaphysics of Christian Science, like the rules of mathematics prove the rule by inversion." She

still further illustrates this by the following:
" There is no pain in Truth, and no truth in
pain ; no nerve in Mind, and no mind in nerve;
no matter in Mind, and no mind in matter; no
matter in Life, and no life in matter; no matter
in Good, and no good in matter." These
astonishing propositions are stated with the
utmost seriousness, and with the dogmatism
and sententiousness of a divine oracle giving
some ex cathedra decision. But how they
prove anything, or, even mean anything, that
is clear and unambiguous, it is difficult to discover.

For example, if the first proposition is interpreted to mean, that " God is all in all," so
as to leave no place for the personality of the
individual, then it denies a fact of human consciousness, which man *knows*, and must know
before he *can* know anything else.

The third proposition is truly "fundamental"
to the whole theory of Christian Science, but
it is opposed not only to Christianity and to
Science, but also to reason and common sense.
It is a dangerous theory because false.

Proposition four is an amazing piece of
assumption. Mrs. Eddy repeats it backward.
It reads equally well either way, as do most
other parts of the book, if taken by paragraphs.
It asserts, that if God is, there is no such thing

as sin, evil, or death; and vice versa, if there is any disease, sin, evil or death, there is no God. Is this true? Is it a fact, that disease, sin, etc., are so incompatible with the nature and purposes of God, that to admit their existence, is to deny the existence of God? There is neither truth, reason, nor logic in such a statement. Mrs. Eddy does not undertake to prove any of her propositions, though she reiterates them in the most positive and dogmatic manner. The Holy Scriptures[2] have considerable to say about sin, evil and death, but Mrs. Eddy has a very unique way of warping them all to suit her theories, by a fanciful and picturesque method of interpretation, which scorns the plain meaning of words, and makes anything mean what she would like to have it mean. When she cannot do this, she does not hesitate to intimate that the Scriptures lie. (Page 517.)

INVERSIONS.

Mrs. Eddy's "inversions," above referred to, afford an illustration of her unique logic. She says "there is no pain in Truth, and no truth in pain." This is specious, but deceptive, because the terms of the inversion are equivocal. What Mrs. Eddy means to affirm, is, that

[2] See Note 2, Appendix. "Christian Science and the Bible."

there is no reality in pain, because there is no pain in truth. But give "truth" the same meaning, in both terms, and if there is any truth in the common experiences of human life, then the falsity of the statement becomes apparent. The crucial words are not univocal in both terms of any of the inversions, they are therefore illogical and misleading.

A REDISCOVERY?

Christian Science claims to be a rediscovery of the power employed by Christ in healing the sick, and of the principles on which He wrought his divine works. Mrs. Eddy says these principles must be accepted and believed in before we can have a right understanding of what true science or true Christianity is. She then goes on to explain the peculiar philosophical theory on which her system is based. It will be essential that we understand something of this before we can at all comprehend what Christian Science claims to be.

BRIEF SUMMARY.

But before we enter upon that let me state just here that in my study of the subject I have come to the conclusion that what is new in Christian Science is not true, and what is true is not new. The only new thing about it is the false metaphysical theory on which it is based, which we shall see is opposed both to reason, and to common sense, and is *dangerous because* false. The power of healing is not new and is partly true. It is a power which was undoubtedly exercised in the primitive church, and there has been no age since in which occasional instances of it cannot be found. Before I conclude I shall endeavor to show that the root principle of this healing power is the same, whether attributed to the bones of saints and martyrs, to the virtue of sacred relics, the odylic force, to magnetism or spiritualism, faith cure, hypnotism or to Christian Science. Of course, Christian Science repudiates this thought, but it is a fact, nevertheless, and can be substantiated.

THE KEYSTONE OF THE SYSTEM.

But let us glance briefly at the philosophy of the movement we are considering. Mrs. Eddy says (page 8); "Christian Science explains all cause and effect as mental, not physical. It lifts the veil of mystery from soul and body. It shows the Scientific relation of man to God, disentangles the interlaced ambiguities of Being and sets free the imprisoned thought; so that we may know, in Divine Science, that the universe, including

man and his divine Principle, is harmonious
and eternal. Science shows that what is
termed *matter* is but the subjective state of
what is here termed *mortal mind*." This expression, "mortal mind," is used to signify
everything visible and invisible, material or
immaterial, save only mind, or God, the all in
all. There is nothing real but mind, which is
immortal, omnipotent and omnipresent. All
else is not. All else is only deception and
illusion, unreal, non-existent. All else only
seems. For want of a better word, Mrs. Eddy
uses what she confesses to be the inadequate
term—"mortal mind"—to express it.

On page 173 she says: "The realm of the
real is spiritual. The opposite of spirit is
matter, and the opposite of the real is the
unreal, or material. Matter is an error of
statement." "Nothing we can say or believe
regarding matter is true, except that matter is
unreal and is therefore belief." "Spirit is the
only substance and consciousness recognized
by Science. The senses oppose this; but there
are no material senses, for matter has no sen-
sation." "All that we term sin, sickness and
death is comprised in a belief in matter."
"Free the mind, therefore, of a belief in
matter, and there will be no such thing as
sin, sickness or death." Such things are only

dreams—delusions, creations of the mortal mind. And yet Christian Science claims to be a method of healing the very material bodies whose existence it denies. As an instance of its utter illogicalness, turn to page 246 of " Science and Health," where it states that it is "mortal mind that convulses matter." But matter is defined as " merely a subjective state of the mortal mind," and "mortal mind " is a non-reality, a nonentity. Yet, how can one nonentity or non-existence convulse another nonentity ? Drugs and medicines are non-entities, and so should not be used to cure physical bodies, which are also nonentities. Food is unreal and has no life-sustaining properties ; it is only a " belief of the mortal mind," which has no existence, and Mrs. Eddy thinks that the time may come when material food will be unnecessary. If Christian Scientists would live without food they could prove the truth of their philosophy. The fact is, that Christian Science seems to have a unique way of using language which regards some-thingness and nothingness as interchangeable terms, either of which it assumes by turns, and both of which it occasionally asserts at the same time.

And yet it calls itself a science. And there are sane and intelligent people whose minds are so confused by the kaleidoscopic gyrations of its cabalistic reasoning, that they become hypnotized, and, being unable to distinguish the true from the false in its philosophy, they settle down into a sort of mental paralysis and accept it all.

When Mrs. Eddy asserts the nothingness of matter she runs her idealism into the bald and barren denial of the common sense of the world. There is nothing like it in even such idealists as Fichte and Berkeley. With them matter was the expression of the idea or intelligence that controlled it. It was not real, in the sense of being self-existent, or in the permanency of its forms, but it was actual. So, when Mrs. Eddy asserts the nothingness of matter she teaches a new philosophy. Starting with the dictum that disease and sickness inhere in matter or in the mental conception of it, it is an easy thing by destroying one to destroy the other also. But universal experience of mankind is against this theory, and even Christian Scientists are compelled to conduct themselves, especially in food and drink and clothing, as if matter was something.

CLAIMS PROVE NOTHING.

Mrs. Eddy adduces no proof of her propositions, but simply begs the whole question, by the most astounding assumptions. Professor Bates says: "Matter is the middle term between God, and the soul is the medium of the divine revelation. The relation of the soul to the body is a figure of the relation of God to the world. He is incarnate in matter, as the soul is incarnate in the body. Matter is not evil. The soul knows and communes with God, through matter."

AN EFFORT AT SELF-DECEPTION.

The philosophy of Christian Science is a denial of every sound principle of reasoning that the world has known. The Christian Scientist rejects all science, except his own. He constructs a world after arbitrary principles of his own, which his own experience tells him is false. He tries to make himself believe that there is no such thing as matter, and yet he eats and drinks and lives like other people, with this self-deception at his heart. Now, whatever may be the immediate effects of this cultivation of mental delusions, it must tend in the long run to a life of unreality, which will issue in a species of mental insanity.

A BAD FORM OF BIGOTRY.

Christian Science also is a bad form of bigotry. It is narrowing and dwarfing in every way. With Science and Health as its Bible, and the Bible as its supplement, it scorns all other knowledge. In fact, all other knowledge, all other education about all material things, is a sham and delusion of the mortal mind. Even now some Christian Scientists are taking their children out of the public schools and starting schools of their own, where children can be as free as possible from the adverse claims of mortal mind upon them.

In Racine, Wisconsin, it is reported, that the Christian Scientists recently petitioned the school board to abolish the study of physiology in the public schools, on the ground that it teaches what is not true, concerning the human body, and thus fosters erroneous and dangerous views of human life.

THE OLD PATH, SAFER.

In opposition to the narrowness of Christian Science stands the old Christianity of Christ and the Gospels, a Christianity of sympathy and of common sense; a religion of faith and love, which looks to God as a Father, who placed man in a world which He had made, and in which man was to work out his salvation, and to grow in grace and in the knowledge of God, as he grew in the knowledge of all his Father's works.

CHAPTER II.

In exposing the errors and absurdities of Christian Science, we must not be unfair, nor deny that there is anything good about it. While we may and ought to expose its evils, yet we need not be blind to that which has won for it the devotion of many earnest people. And again, while we condemn its philosophy and its theology as false and dangerous, yet we may admit that its protest against extreme materialism and intellectual pride, is at least most timely. In its practical teaching, the emphasis which it places upon the fact that close dependence on God will lift human life above all care, and worry, and anxiety, is a truth which the Christian religion has always taught, but which very few Christians have tried to realize as they ought. Another lesson which we might learn from it, is the great stress placed upon another old truth, that the secret of godliness is the secret of health.

While we may freely admit all that is good and true about Christian Science, yet on the other hand we ought not to be blind to its evils and untruths. Our purpose is to point out some of these latter, in order to show Christian people that they need not leave their own churches in order to embrace all that is true in Christian Science, nor need they accept its falsehoods and delusions in order to share in all the helpfulness and partake of all the ' powers which Christ came to reveal.

CHRISTIAN SCIENCE, NEITHER CHRISTIAN NOR SCIENTIFIC.

Saint Paul wrote some very good advice to Timothy, which is quite up to date, and pertinent to the question before us. He said: 1 Timothy vi. 20: "O, Timothy, keep that which is committed to thy trust, avoiding profane and vain babblings and oppositions of science, falsely so-called, which some professing have erred concerning the faith."

A very little study of history will reveal that it was something similar to Christian Science, which the apostle had in mind, when he wrote these words, and a very little study of Christian Science will reveal that both as to its Christianity, and its science, it is "falsely so-called."

The term Christian has a clear and distinct meaning. A Christian is one who believes in Jesus Christ, as revealed in the Gospels, accepts his message and tries to obey his commands. Now, it is true that those who call themselves Christian Scientists, do speak of Jesus Christ with great reverence, but the Christ of Christian Science is not the Christ of the Gospels, but an entirely new invention evolved from the fertile brain of Mrs. Eddy. I say new, and yet not new, either, save in one particular, since her Jesus Christ is a poorly digested mixture and recrudescence of a number of old heresies, which she has revamped and set forth as a new revelation. It is only by an entire perversion and disregard of the plain meaning of words and the whole teaching of the Christian centuries that the Christianity of Mrs. Eddy can be shown to have any identity with the Christianity of Christ and his apostles. Her "Science and Health," page 478, speaks of Jesus as "the highest human concept of a perfect man," and yet page 229 as only a "human corporeal concept." Page 358 speaks of Him as knowing "the mortal error which constitutes the material body," but intimates that He was less free from error and less true in this respect than Mrs. Mary Baker Eddy, in that He "had not conquered all the beliefs of the flesh, or his sense of material life."

We shall refer to the teachings of Christian

Science about Jesus Christ again when we come to speak of its theology. But for a religion to call itself " Christian," which has no clear conception of a personal God, which denies the incarnation, which knows no sin and recognizes no need of a Saviour—for such a system to call itself Christian is either a confession of ignorance on the part of those who do it, or an appeal to the ignorance of others.

The same argument applies to the assumption of the word "science," as a part of its name.[3] I think it was the Duke of Argyle who defined science as a "systematic knowledge of phenomena or facts in their relation to other facts, and to ourselves." A scientist, therefore, is one who has attained such scientific knowledge in some branch of scientific research. Putting the two words together, and a Christian Scientist is a person who, in addition to his scientific knowledge, is also an open and avowed Christian. But can you tell me of any scientist, whether Christian or unbeliever, who has accepted the theories and opinions of Mrs. Eddy? I have yet to hear of even one single one of any reputable standing who has done so. Mrs. Eddy says in the preface to her book that "no intellectual proficiency is required in the learner" of her sci-

[3] See Note 3, Appendix.   Mrs. Eddy's " Science."

ence. (I make no comments.) The name is
an entire misnomer.

THE NAME, A BID FOR POPULARITY.

Mr. P. T. Barnum used to say that "people
like to be humbugged." The term "science"
sounds well and is taking in the ears of this
generation, which is eager to follow any one
who professes to have a knowledge beyond
the range of common men, and helps to fool
some, who are not piously inclined, and with
"Christian" prefixed, the name helps to fool
others, who are piously inclined, but who want
to find some new and easier, or more exciting
method of serving God. It may seem ungen-
erous, yet I can but think that the name was
a shrewd bid for popularity, and is falsely applied to "Christian Science," because it denies
nearly all the accepted tenets of Christianity,
as taught in the Catholic faith, and opposes
nearly all the precepts on which the science
of the world is based.

ILLOGICAL CONCLUSIONS.

There are many intelligent people, who
seem to lack logical perception, just as some
are wanting in color perception, and are what
we call color blind. This fact forms one of
the secrets of the success of the Christian

Science movement. For example, it is often claimed that the cures which Christian Science undoubtedly effects are "demonstrations"* of its truth, since, as its adherents are fond of quoting, "by their fruits ye shall know them." But sacred shrines⁴ and the bones of saints, have wrought cures, as remarkable as any that Christian Science can boast of. Does this prove that shrines and saints' bones contain the divine principle? Faith cure, magnetism, hypnotism, and a dozen other systems, also heal cases, after their methods, equally wonderful, but does their "demonstration" of the power to heal, prove the truth of any or all of their conflicting theories?

The only demonstration there is—is that they all can heal certain classes of disease, and the fact is, whatever their theory about it may be, that the principle by which the cure is effected, is the same in them all, whether they know or believe it or whether they do not. Almost any person, after a little instruction and practice, can heal as well as any Christian Scientist.

But Christian Scientists, in their desire to make it appear that they have a *monopoly* of the method or principle of healing which

* Preface to Science and Health, page viii.
⁴ See Note 4, Appendix.   Shrine of Bishop Neuman.

Jesus used, frantically denounce all other methods. Yet Jesus Himself said that it was no proof of anything distinctively Christian about either the system or the method of those who assumed the title, that they claimed to work cures in his name. He declared, "many will say unto Me in that day, Lord, Lord, have we not prophesied in thy name? and in thy name have cast out devils? and in thy name done many wonderful works? and then will I profess unto them, I never knew you: depart from Me, ye that work iniquity " (*i. e.*, without law). Matt. vii. 22.

CABALISTIC.

The same sort of illogicalness applies to the cures and conversions wrought by reading Mrs. Eddy's book. Its peculiar effect upon the minds of those who are led to take it up from sickness or intellectual unrest, is often thought to be a "demonstration" of its truth. But the fact is that these persons are confused by the circuitous convolutions of its inconsequential reasoning, its constant suppression of half truths, and its astounding assumptions, until they become bewildered and hypnotized, and are ready to accept anything that Mrs. Eddy says, because the book so boldly and confidently affirms that Mrs. Eddy *knows*.

The word hypnotized is used purposely, since this is the essential principle which underlies the whole scheme. Science and Health is largely made up of cabalistic utterances, which on close examination mean nothing clear and definite, but which are claimed to be momentously full of some mysterious and occult significance, which to those who can discover it, will be the revelation of divine truth—or divine science. This is practically a cabalistic method of hypnotizing. Christian Science healers, who seek to heighten the mystery by continued silence, and the repetition of similar mystic utterances, work on the same principle.

CHAPTER III.

THE PHILOSOPHY OF CHRISTIAN SCIENCE, DANGEROUS AND IMMORAL.

In order to understand Christian Science, it will be necessary to examine it under three heads, and see what it is, as to its philosophy, its theology, and its therapeutics. The first is the most fundamental, since it is the key to its peculiar theology, and explains the theory upon which its therapeutics was constructed. We have already referred to the uniqueness of its philosophy, in the absolute denial of matter.

Now the more thoroughly this is understood, not only the more absurd, but the more dangerous will it be seen to be, in its influences both on the intellectual and the moral life.

Let us glance at these two points. In the first place, Christian Science is an intellectual sin.

AN INTELLECTUAL SIN, AND LOGICAL COMEDY.

It is a deliberate prostitution and debasement of the human reason by the cultivation of a delusion. Its adherents make believe that there is no such thing as matter, that every material thing is only an "erroneous belief of the mortal mind." Mortal mind is a nothingness, and so matter *is an erroneous belief of one nothingness in another nothingness.* Now, this is a dangerous mental heresy, and tends to intellectual bankruptcy. Yet their whole system is founded on it. It is the very groundwork of science and health. Mrs. Eddy's scheme stands or falls with it.

But what is the basis on which Christian Scientists profess to believe in the absolute non-existence of matter? Their whole experience is against their theory and the common sense of the world denies it, and the only reason which can be adduced is that "Mother Eddy says so." Observe that I am not objecting to the fact that intelligence is the reality below all phenomena, that mind has .power over matter, but to the absolute denial of any actuality to matter. Take a practical point. Mrs. Eddy says (" Science and Health," page 387), "Admit the common hypothesis that food is what sustains life, and there follows the necessity for another admission in the opposite direction, namely, that food has power to destroy life, through its deficiency or excess in quality or quantity." "If mortals think that food disturbs the harmonious functions of mind and body, either the food or this thought must be dispensed with. If this decision be not destroyed, it may some day say that they are dying from want of food."

Yet Christian Scientists feed their non-existent bodies, which are only "illusions" and "false claims of the mortal mind" with other "illusions" and "false claims of the mortal mind," which also have no existence—called food—just the same as other people do, all the time that they profess to believe that they have no bodies and that there is no such thing as food, save as "erroneous beliefs of the mortal mind." So, to express it very mildly, I say this is an intellectual sin, a mental heresy, a debasement of the human reason, which is one of God's greatest gifts to man.

Then see the comedy of this logic in its effect on civilization. If Mrs. Eddy says true in her denial of matter, then there is no use in schools to teach children to read, because all books, even "Science and Health," with its key to the Bible, are only "delusions." There is no use in studying such "erroneous beliefs" as mathematics and botany and chemistry nor anything else. Better close up all our schools and colleges and institutions of learning, and shut up all shops and stores and cease all physical labor—to provide food and everything else—so that mankind may just give itself up to meditation on divine science—as revealed by Mrs. Eddy—where mind can feed on mind and enjoy the supreme felicity of its own everlasting oneness and allness. This, it seems to me, is the plain logical issue to which the philosophy of Christian Science would lead us.

A FORMULA FOR IMMORALITY.

Now, it may appear invidious and uncharitable and even malicious to assert that the philosophical theory on which Christian Science rests, has a direct tendency to foster and encourage immorality and crime. While bearing witness to the fact that Christian Scientists, as far as I know them, do try to live pure, upright and beautiful lives, lives that just now manifest more of that sense of closeness to God than the lives of ordinary Christians do, yet, in spite of this, I assert that its philosophy is immoral, and will tend in the long run to encourage vice and crime.[5] Mrs. Eddy says " An error in the premises must appear in the conclusion," and, that " incorrect reasoning leads to practical error." In this she is quite correct. On page 444 she tries to guard against the " practical error," to which her own

[5] See Note 5, Appendix. (A system of deception.)

reasoning leads, by saying, "A sinner is not reformed merely by assuring him that he cannot be a sinner, because there is no sin. To put down the claim of sin you must detect it, remove the mask, point out the illusion, and thus get the victory over sin and prove its unreality." Now, not to dwell upon the fact that Mrs. Eddy contradicts herself in her use of the word sin, the point I desire to emphasize is that, if "the soul cannot sin," if sin is only an error of the mortal mind, then the practical outcome of this theory will surely be that man, being spiritual, his nature cannot be corrupted by anything his mortal mind can do, by any immoralities he may indulge in. Christian Scientists may deny this—I am quite sure they would most deeply deplore it —but Mr. Max Müller said that "history is a truer, though, perhaps, a sterner, teacher than any theory."

AN APPEAL TO HISTORY.

Christian Science is a new religion, and is seeking just now, as new religions always do, to justify itself before the world by the high living of its members. So I appeal to history to show how a precisely similar theory has led to error in Gnosticism. Dr. Waterman in his recent history of the apostolic age, says " the

Gnostics held that man was dragged down by the imprisonment of his spirit in his body. Deliver him from that bondage and he would soon and easily be perfected." "The two notions" (bear in mind that Dr. Waterman is speaking of Gnosticism, not of Christian Science), "the two notions that knowledge is salvation, and that matter is an evil which must be shaken off as a condition of passing into a higher state of being, led some high-minded men to devote themselves nobly to plain living and high thinking. Some of the Gnostic founders were certainly men of devotion and self-denial. But frequently the followers of such leaders ran, after a generation or so, into depths of licentious immorality. They said "the body was an evil thing, anyhow, why try to keep it from doing evil things?" The only course for a true Gnostic was to let his body do as it would, and keep his soul proudly apart, well aware that it was a separate organism, with a distinct character of its own now, and a distinct destiny of its own hereafter." Dr. Waterman speaks of this as "a doctrine of practical corruption." So, after the novelty of Mrs. Eddy's theory has worn off, I can readily see how her formula, that the body is nothing, and cannot corrupt the soul, will be used as a cloak to cover shameless im-

morality and extreme self-indulgence.   Mrs.
Eddy's "incorrect reasoning" is sure to lead
"to practical error."

ITS THEOLOGY.

As to the theology of Christian Science in
general, it is not easy to speak, since its language is so vague and unscientific and its reasoning so fragmentary and disjointed that it is
difficult to tell just what is taught.   Then, too,
the Scriptures are appealed to and interpreted
in such an eccentric way, and their plain and
manifest meaning is warped and perverted to
suit their peculiar theories, so that one can
scarcely recognize them.[2]   But the Christian
Science idea of God is unmistakably pantheistic.   The writings of their doctors and
teachers are rank with pantheism.   In fair-
ness, however, I will say that I do not think
they intend to teach this.   What they aim
at, is the doctrine of Divine Immanence, but
in Mrs. Eddy's absolute denial of matter,
and in her eagerness to avoid materialistic
pantheism, she runs headlong to the other extreme and lands flat in spiritual pantheism,
which is no better.   I am well aware that they
all vehemently deny this, but what does this
denial amount to when you can confront them

[2] See Note 2, Appendix.   "Christian Science and the Bible."

with the deadly witness of their own testimony. For example, "Science and Health," page 226, says, "God is Spirit, and Spirit is divine Principle." "Nothing possesses reality or existence except Mind, God, who is all in all." "Everything in God's universe, His is idea." Page 225, "God is supreme Being, the only Life, Substance and Soul, the only Intelligence of the universe, including man."

At times Mrs. Eddy speaks of God in terms of personality, but the prevailing trend of Science and Health sets forth God in impersonal and abstract terms, which admit of no personality, of which "principle" seems to predominate. I have not time to multiply quotations, but I submit that the whole trend of "Science and Health," is pantheistic. The God of Christian Science is more like the Brahma of Hindu mythology, than the God whom Christ revealed and taught us to worship. Their favorite expression for God is "Principle." He is not a person, a father who hears and answers prayer, for we are told that "prayer to a personal God is a hindrance."

As to its teaching about Jesus Christ the same pantheistic taint runs through this also. Mrs. Eddy says, "Christ is the idea of truth, and this idea comes to heal sickness and sin." Jesus, however, is different from the Christ.

Jesus was a "human concept," born of the
Virgin, the Virgin's Son, while Christ was
God's Son, his "spiritual and eternal idea."
(Pages 228 and 229.) Yet the two were joined
in some occult way by the union of the divine
idea with the man Jesus. It was the Virgin's
Son, who was man. "He appeared to men in
such form of humanity as they could understand and perceive." But his body was only
an appearance, "an error of the mortal mind,"
a delusion to which He lent Himself. Therefore, the crucifixion was an unreality, the pas-
sion an illusion, and his sacrifice for sin, a
delusion. Christian Science has no place for
sin. It is only "a false belief." Its existence
"denies God," (page 7). As man is a part of
God, he is "incapable of sin," (page 476). The
soul cannot sin, (pages 464, etc.).

But why pursue the thought further? I can
only say, that a more dreary swamp of metaphysical contradictions or a cruder conglomer-
ation of exploded theological heresies than
Christian Science offers I have never seen.
Jesus taught us to pray, saying, "Our Father,"
but Christian Science turns Our Father into
"a principle," and why pray to a "principle."

St. Paul preached Jesus Christ and Him
crucified, yea, risen from the dead, but Christian Science teaches us that our Lord was an

"idea," " which dwells forever in the bosom of the Father," (page 229).

Mrs. Eddy says we cannot sin because sin is only an erroneous belief of the mortal mind, but St. John, the disciple whom Jesus loved, said, " If we say that we have no sin, we deceive ourselves, and the truth is not in us."

We need to-day to heed the admonition of St. Paul to "keep that which is committed to our trust." The Catholic faith has been the church's safeguard from errors in the past, and we need to hold fast to its everlasting truths to guard us from the fascinating delusions of all falsely-called sciences or religions of to-day. "Keep that which is committed to thy trust," and you can be sure that the old faith and the old religion which alone have met the wants of men in the past and have stood unshaken by heresies nigh 2,000 years, will alone be able to meet the real needs of men in the present, and to preserve the " truth as it is in Jesus " for the wants of 2,000 years to come."

" If thou put the brethren in remembrance of these things, thou shalt be a good minister of Jesus Christ, nourished up in the words of faith and of good doctrine, whereunto thou hast attained. But refuse profane and old wives' fables, and exercise thyself rather unto godliness."—1 Timothy iv. 6 and 7.

CHAPTER IV.

MENTAL HEALING EXPLAINED.

In endeavoring to follow the admonition of St. John, to "try the spirits, whether they are of God," we have examined the spirit of Christian Science, as to its philosophy, and found it opposed to the common sense of the world, and its theory likely to prove a formula for corruption. We have glanced at its theology, and found its idea of God, a spiritual pantheism, contrary to the plain meaning of the Holy Scriptures, as the Christian world has always received and interpreted them. Its doctrines about Jesus Christ, are in one sense novel, and present Him as a new invention of Mrs. Eddy, although in another sense, they can be shown to be only a recrudescence and fresh mixture of a number of old and exploded heresies.

METHODS OF DISARMING CRITICISM.

While we have tried to be fair in our criticisms of Christian Science, and to state nothing which is not true, yet we have not hesitated to speak plainly, and to condemn its manifest errors and absurdities. Yet there are two stock phrases which Christian Scientists use, to answer all unfavorable and disparaging criticisms. The first is that of "ignorance." They say the critic has never had a revelation of the "Divine Principle," "he does not know what Christian Science is," and therefore "is incompetent to speak of it." The second, is the cry of "persecution."

As to the first, it is a confession of the vagueness and mysticism of their system, which uses words in such various and fanciful senses, that it requires a special illumination to know what they mean. But any one who has studied Christian Science, and kept his mind clear from its bewildering confusions of thought, can with equal truth and with better reason assert, that those whose minds have become imbued (hypnotized) with its occult phrases, do not themselves really understand the significance of the system in which they profess to believe.

As to the charge of "persecution," the Christian Science movement, in organizing a new church, and setting itself up as a new sect and practically inviting Christian people to leave their own churches and become Christian Scientists, naturally and necessarily invites criticism of the principles on which it is founded. While practically teaching that their own system is the true, and only true one, it seems to me something like cant for them to assume a rôle of injured innocence, and claim that they are being persecuted for truth's sake, when the falseness of their theories is shown up.

ANOTHER PLEA.

Yet some of them simply say, " Why not let us alone ? " " If we find peace in Christian Science, why disturb us with adverse criticisms ? " Why indeed ? Why criticise or object to any untruths or false theories, if people enjoy them ? Why condemn any evil systems or delusions, so long as there is some good in them ? The simple reason is, that untruths in theory are sure to lead to untruths in practice.

A LOST HERITAGE.

That which first drew attention to Christian Science, and has helped more than anything else to win for it the place it holds in the popular mind, is its system of mental or metaphysical healing. In this, it calls our attention to a lost heritage of the Christian Church; but the question is, *is it desirable for us to regain it ?* Now, there is no doubt that the healing of bodily diseases was a part of the ministry of our Lord. His mission was to the whole man. Nor again, is there any doubt that the apostles possessed and exercised the power of healing, and considered it a part of their mission. St. Matthew x. 1-8, records that Jesus called his twelve disciples "and gave them authority over unclean spirits to cast them out, and to heal all manner of disease and all manner of sickness." When He sent them out to preach the Gospel of the kingdom He said to them, "Heal the sick, raise the dead, cleanse the lepers, etc." That the disciples exercised this power is evident from the story of their labors in the Book of Acts. The third chapter tells of the healing of the lame man at the Beautiful gate, by Peter and John. The eighth chapter of Acts mentions that when Philip went down to preach Christ at Samaria, "Many that were palsied and lame were healed." Acts ix. 33, contains records of the cure of Eneas, who had kept his bed for eight years. Acts xiv. 9, bears witness that at Lystra Paul cured "a certain man impotent in his feet, a cripple from his mother's womb, who had never walked."

SPECIAL INSTANCES.

There are some instances which deserve especial attention, as showing that the presence of the healer was not always necessary in order to effect the cure. The Gospels mention four cases, where Jesus healed at a distance, even without the knowledge on their part that He was about to do so. Acts v. 15, states that the shadow of Peter passing by cured multitudes, both of men and women, and Acts xix. 12, testifies that when handkerchiefs or aprons were carried to the sick from St. Paul, "The diseases departed from them." This leaves no doubt that the original disciples of our Lord regarded the healing of the bodies of men as a part of their ministry. Nor was this gift confined to the first disciples. The epistles effectually settle that it was not, and history establishes the fact that for well-nigh 300 years gifts of healing seem to have been exercised in the church. But gradually the power seems to have died out, or Christians neglected its use, until it was no longer considered a sign of the indwelling spirit, and at last even the consciousness of its possession faded from the church at large. Yet here and there through the centuries there are occasional reappearances of the power. But the notion became prevalent that the gift of healing was an exceptional gift—vouchsafed only for the peculiar emergencies of the early days of the church, as a special evidence of its divine mission, though there is no intimation in the New Testament, to warrant any such conclusion.

A SUGGESTIVE TENDENCY.

Now it is evident to any one who has watched the various forms of mental therapeutics which have arisen during the past generation, that most of them are religious in their character, and indicate a tendency to return to a belief in the double mission of the Gospel as Jesus taught it and his disciples practiced it. This is suggestive of a great truth, which both the wise priest and the wise physician will do well to ponder—because at least some diseases are the result of sins, and some sins the result of disease, so that to save from one it is sometimes necessary to cure the other.

THE METHODS OF JESUS.

Let me say a word here as to the methods of healing which Jesus employed, as explanatory of something later. As we examine the cures wrought by Jesus, they can be arranged under four heads. First, those in which He simply spake the word—such as to the blind man, "receive thy sight," or to the man with the withered arm, "stretch forth thy hand," or to the impotent man at Bethesda, "Arise, take up thy couch, and walk." The second class of cures are such as in addition to the spoken word Jesus had recourse to personal touch, when He laid his hands on people and they recovered. This would seem to be his usual custom, since those who came to Him, as a rule, besought Him, like the centurion, to " come and *lay thine hands* on her, that she may be healed."

The third class of cures were those wrought at a distance, to which I have already referred, and the fourth, those in which Jesus resorted to the use of material means, as when He anointed the eyes of a blind man with clay mingled with saliva, or when He put saliva on the tongue, and his fingers in the ears of one who was deaf and dumb.

THE PRINCIPLE, THE SAME.

Yet on careful study, in the light of recent knowledge, the principle which underlies them all is the same, and the variation in method was adopted simply because He, who knew the temperament of each, probably adopted the method by which the result could be best attained. I have mentioned these instances in order to lead up to the principle which underlies the power of healing, which has undoubtedly been exercised by many in the past, and is also exercised by many to-day. Now, in speaking of the cures wrought by Jesus, it has been the custom to regard them as supernatural and call them miracles, as if Jesus wrought them solely as the Son of God. Yet there is nothing in the New Testament to support this view. Jesus came, as perfect man, to reveal the powers which belong to perfect manhood. He had no thought of any exclusive use of his power to heal, nor even to forgive sins. He said the first should belong to all that believed, and to his disciples He said: "Whosesoever sins ye remit, they are remitted unto them."

THE POWER OF HEALING, THE BIRTHRIGHT OF MAN.

As I mentioned above, the history of the first three centuries proves that it was not his purpose to have men regard the power of healing as exclusively a *divine power*, but rather as something revealed by Him as a birthright of man, God's child; a natural power, natural to the true nature of man, whom God made in his own image, and in whom He breathed a portion of his own spirit. In man's ignorance of his own spiritual self he has been in the habit of calling everything he could not understand miraculous, and attribut-

ing it to some special intervention of God, or
of the devil. I propose to show that it is
only on account of ignorance of our spiritual
selves, our lack of knowledge of the marvelous
soul forces which God has given us, that we
do so. If we believed more fully in Jesus ,
Christ, we should believe that a part of his
mission was to reveal man to himself, in order
that he might know that his true life was a
life indwelt by the spirit of God, and that
with God nothing was impossible.

We have made but little progress in the
knowledge of ourselves for many centuries.
Our attention has been diverted to things
physical and material. But just at the height
of our materialism, when man had claimed to
find thought forces in the grey matter of the
brain, and his origin in protoplastic cells, the
providence of God turned our attention to the
study of the inner spiritual man, and led him
to find in psychic forces the real forces which
make and control the life of man. Psychology
is practically a new science, and its recent
revelations have been among the most startling and wonderful discoveries of this wonderful age.

PSYCHIC FORCES CONTROL FUNCTIONS.

Let us apply some of these to the special

question now before us in their relation to disease and its cure. The ancient wise man of Israel said: "As a man thinketh in his heart, so is he." There is a profounder truth here than the world has yet recognized. Medical men are beginning to declare that the mind is the most potent factor in nearly all physical ills. Some one has said: "We feel as we think we feel. If we think we feel pain, we feel pain; if we think we feel sick, we are sick." I am not speaking of merely imaginary ills, but of the power of the imagination to exercise a real though unconscious control over the functions of the body. The books tell us that in experiments medical students who imagine they are bleeding to death grow weak and faint, and that one student actually died, when only warm water was spurted over an imagined incision in an artery in his arm. Fear will not only blanch the hair, but will paralyze the heart and stop its healthy action. The sight of an accident has thrown persons into spasms from which they have died, and has often given to nervous people a shock from which they have never recovered. Dr. Schofield, of the Royal College of Surgeons, England, says that "not only functional and organic diseases are caused by the mind, but that death itself is quite common." I might give you page

after page of instances from reputable books
and medical journals which prove beyond
gainsay that the mind not only produces
certain diseases, but that it also is important
in determining the effect of many medicines,
and that bread pills or a little powdered sugar
—or even plain water—would often produce
the effect which the doctor had led the patient
to believe it would produce.   Dr. Schofield
says that the symptoms of many diseases can
be produced in a patient by the simple suggestion of them; that the surest way to be
attacked by any infectious disease is to be
afraid of it, because the mind can induce the
symptoms of diseases by thinking about them.
I could bring you other testimony from noted
physicians to the same effect.

THE SECRET REVEALED.

Now, this is the remarkable discovery I
referred to which has recently been made,
viz, that as the mind can undoubtedly cause
many diseases, unconsciously to itself, so it has
been ascertained, that *if the impression of
disease can be removed from the mind the
disease itself will very often entirely dis-
appear.*   This is the root principle which lies
at the foundation of all mental therapeutics.
This is the secret of all the cures wrought by

the various methods of healing, whether by the
Christian Science method or the faith-healing
method, by the magnetic or a dozen others.
They are all simply different methods of re-
lieving the unconscious mind of the impression
of disease and implanting in its place the impression of ease and hope and health. Christian
Science does this by impressing the mind with
the idea of the non-existence of any disease,
by denying the existence of matter. This is
one theory, but it is based on a falsehood and
is opposed to the common sense of the world.
Faith cure has another theory and magnetic
healing another, and so on, but the principle un-
derneath them all is the same. Now, you may
find a key which will fit one door of a house,
and it may be simply a coincidence, but if it
fits and unlocks all the doors you are justified
in thinking you have the master-key. Such is
the principle whose action I will now try to
explain as briefly as I can. If any of you
have read Dr. Hudson's "Law of Psychic
Phenomena" you have the explanation more
in detail. In a few words, it is practically
this: Indirect investigation of psychic conditions induced by hypnotism has established
the fact that we possess *two minds*. Dr.
Hudson calls them the objective and the subjective minds.

THE TWO MINDS.

Dr. Schofield speaks of them as the conscious and the unconscious mind, others refer to the latter as the soul—and others still as the subliminal self. In ordinary sleep, when the conscious mind is dormant, the unconscious mind continues active. Dreams are an evidence of this. Now it is found that the unconscious mind, or soul, while apparently incapable of inductive reasoning, is the seat of the memory and the affections, and also has the power to control the functions of the body. As a rule it receives its impressions from, and is under the control and guidance of the conscious or objective mind with which it is associated, but it is also capable of acting independently. Now it has been found that if the direction and guidance of one's own objective mind is removed or placed in abeyance, or rendered passive by sleep, which is what hypnotism is—or in any other way, then the subjective mind will receive impressions and accept almost implicitly the direction and guidance of the objective mind of another. In the hypnotic or sleep condition the patient has as much confidence in the objective mind that controls him as he has in his own. If the hypnotizer assures him that a lead pencil is a steam engine, or that a chair is the President of the United States, the mind receives the image suggested. The way this is applied to the cure of disease is simply this. The physician has a patient suffering from any disease who wants to be healed. The desire to be healed predisposes to faith. If the healer finds that the patient has perfect faith in what he says, then the subjective mind will receive the suggestion awake, about as readily as when asleep. And the differences in method are simply different ways of securing this faith, or the yielding of the subjective mind to receive the suggestion of the healer. This is essential in all. The patient may not be aware himself that he is yielding, but until he does so nothing can be done. The secret is always—*if thou believest, thou canst be healed.* But when the subjective mind is secured, then the suggestion is implanted, that there is no pain or sickness—or that it has gone, and "as a person thinketh, so is he." Of course, in deep seated or chronic cases immediate cure is not suggested, or not attained, but only gradual improvement, and the treatment requires frequent repetitions of the "suggestion."

TESTIMONY OF PHYSICIANS.

Dr. Woods, medical superintendent of Hoxton House Asylum, England, says he has treated over 1,000 cases by suggestion, and finds it a most potent remedy, not only in functional, but in organic troubles.* Dr. Reed, of Cincinnati, says he has seen it relieve pain more speedily than morphine, and that he has seen it induce sleep more quickly than chloroform.† A prominent physician of this city tells me that he has performed painful operations simply by suggesting to the patient, while in the hypnotic condition, that he would feel nothing, and the operation was painless. Another physician of this city tells me that he has used suggestion, in hundreds of cases, both in the sleeping and waking condition, and also at a distance, with results which if he had mentioned them ten years ago, would have caused him to be considered the rankest kind of a lunatic. He says he can cure by this method any case whatever, that any Christian Scientist on earth can cure; and he also tells me, having made a professional study of psychic laws, that I am perfectly correct in stating that the principle is the same, whether those who practice it, know it or do not know it, and whether the method is called Christian Science or Faith Cure, or Scriptural Healing,

* Journal Society for Psychical Research, 1897.
† Medical Mirror, Feb. 1, 1899.

or Divine Healing, or Magnetic Healing; whether the cure be attributed to bones of saints, the holy coat at Treves, the grotto at Lourdes, the King's touch, or to charms or idols.

PEOPLE OF ONE IDEA, DANGEROUS.

Christian Scientists, of course, deny this, but a careful examination has convinced me absolutely, that the secret of the cures in all these methods is scientifically explained by the wonderful control of the soul or unconscious mind over the functions and processes of the body.   I have no time to mention the deductions from this psychic law, as they relate to what is called " auto-suggestion," or the power one has to cure one's self.   All wise physicians are recognizing and making use of it, and will probably do so more and more.   But people of one idea are always dangerous.   Doctors who believe in the wonderful power of the soul or unconscious mind over the body, say they have yet to hear of a dislocated or broken bone suggested into place or wholeness, or a well-developed case of cancer, and various other diseases, suggested away.[6]   There are always two sides to every question, and while the

<hr>

[6] Note Appendix.   The Christian Science theory, breaks at its strongest point.

powers of the mind over the body may lead
some to think that the mind is all, and alone
important, yet it is also well to remember that
the body also is a radical part of man in this
present state of existence, and has direct relation to and influence upon the mind. Materia
medica has a place in psychology as well as in
physiology, and will continue side by side in
the practice of the wise physician.

SHALL THE CHURCH ENDEAVOR TO REGAIN ITS LOST HERITAGE?

Now shall the church endeavor to regain its
lost heritage, and the clergy return again to
the healing of the body as a part of their
Christian ministry? I have not the slightest
doubt that with a little practice they could all
do so, as well as Christian Scientists. Would
it be wise? In exceptional cases it might be,
but I am constrained to believe that the best
plan is for the clergyman to know his own
business and to coöperate with the physician,
and I believe it is also the part of the wise
physician to recognize the aid that a discreet
clergyman can render, especially in critical
cases. *The evolution of history is the out-
working of God, and changed methods may be
an indication of an advance in His purposes.*
The greater knowledge required to-day in

ministering to the salvation of mankind, indi-
cates that a division of labor may be of divine
ordering, and that physicians are as truly
called of God to their part of the ministry of
saving men, as the clergy are to theirs, and
that it is not wise to combine the two again.
One profession is about all that a man can well
attend to. The sad story of the death of
Harold Frederic illustrates what I mean.[7]
When stricken with paralysis, the condition of
his heart was such that he needed rest and
quiet. Physicians said that his life could undoubtedly have been prolonged. But he came
under the influence of Christian Scientists
who were ignorant of those physiological laws
which the researches and experience of centuries have established, and they encouraged
him to walk and drive and go about, just as if
"nothing was the matter." As usual, the
healers were unwilling to consult with the
doctors; they must have the whole direction
or none at all. So he went about under the
direction of Christian Scientists, as if "nothing was the matter," and the sad result[8] you
all know. Now, this illustrates the danger in
treating according to any psychic method, by
those who have no education in anatomy and

[7] See note, Appendix. What can be done?
[8] See Appendix, note 8. The most devoted adherents.

physiology, and who repudiate the experience and common sense of the centuries in their devotion to any one "idea-ism" which a restless age may offer.

CONCLUSION.

To conclude, while Christian Science has much that is beautiful and attractive, yet I say that all of it can be attained just as well in the church by those who will seek it. I must say, also, that I can but think that some Christian Scientists are deceived, and mistake the playing at metaphysics for the cultivation of spirituality. My advice to all is, not to be carried away by the fascination of the new "ism." Its *philosophy is dangerous, its theology is heresy, and its therapeutics is quackery.* Although your soul may hunger for some new and more spicy food to feed its spiritual longings, yet I say this—that if you use faithfully (*i. e.*, with faith) and earnestly the means which Christ has appointed in his church, you will surely find them ample to minister to your soul's truest needs, and to guide your feet in ways of peace, here and forever.

APPENDIX.

Note 1.

Mrs. Eddy's "Revelation."

An article in the *Arena* for May, 1899, contains almost conclusive evidence, that Mrs. Eddy was indebted for her "revelation" of the theory of Mental Healing, to Dr. P. P. Quimby, of Portland, Maine, to whom she formerly went for treatment. The article claims that neither the name, "Christian Science," nor that of her book "Science and Health," were original with her.

See also, "True History of Christian Science," by J. A. Dresser.

Note 2.

Christian Science and the Bible

CHRISTIAN Scientists profess to respect the Bible, but a more wretched perversion of its whole meaning, "mortal mind" never conceived. The ordinary Christian would fail to recognize even the Lord's Prayer, under Mrs. Eddy's interpretation. It reads as follows, and is used in Christian Science Services (page 322).

> Our Father which art in Heaven,
> *Our Father and Mother God, all-harmonious,*

Hallowed be Thy name.
> *Adorable one.*

Thy Kingdom come.
> *Thy Kingdom is come,*
> *God is ever-present and omnipotent.*

Thy will be done in earth, as it is in Heaven.
> *Enable us to know—as in Heaven, so on earth—God is*
> *All in all.*

Give us this day our daily bread;
> *Give us grace for to-day; feed Thou the famished affec-*
> *tions.*

And forgive us our debts, as we forgive our debtors.
> *And divine Love is reflected in love;*

And lead us not into temptation, but deliver us from evil;
> *And leaveth us not in temptation, but delivereth us from*
> *evil—sin, disease, and death.*

For Thine is the Kingdom and the power and the glory
forever.
> *For God is omnipresent Good, Substance, Life, Truth,*
> *Love.*

As a sample of Mrs. Eddy's picturesque method of exegesis and the playfulness of her etymology, note the following (page 233).

"The word Adam is from the Hebrew *Adamah*, signifying the *red color of the ground, dust, nothingness.* Divide the name Adam into two syllables, and it reads, *a dam* or obstruction. This suggests the thought of something fluid, of mortal mind in solution, etc." Yet there are people who take Mrs. Eddy seriously, and really believe that her phrases mean something.

Let any one read her "Exegesis," pages 496 to 517, and he will find that she becomes so entangled in the jumble of her mystic and fanciful interpretations, that in order to extricate herself, she is obliged to assert that the second chapter of Genesis, "is a lie" (page 517). The key to the Bible would be amusing, were it not pitiful.

Note 3.

Mrs. Eddy's Science.

As an example of the scientific character of Mrs. Eddy's mind, and her (in)capacity for accurate observation, note the following astounding passage. Science and Health page 549. "It is related that a father, anxious to try such an experiment, plunged his infant babe, only a few hours old, into water for several minutes, and repeated this operation daily, until the child could remain under water twenty minutes, moving and playing without harm, like a fish."

Let any one put a newborn babe under the water even for *one* minute, and if the "awakening of the mortal mind," (which Mrs. Eddy speaks of, in the previous paragraph) ever comes to that child, it will assuredly be in the "Spiritual Life," unless artificially restored. The value of Mrs. Eddy's *scientific* observations can be readily estimated.

Note 4.

Shrine of Bishop Neuman.

PHILADELPHIA, PA., November 17, 1898.—The fame of the miracles wrought at the tomb of Bishop Neuman in St. Peter's Church, Fifty-eighth street and Girard avenue, continues to grow, with the result that every day the number of pilgrims to the shrine increases. The fathers say that the number in a day reaches into the hundreds.

From far and near the people come, afflicted with various ailments, each hoping that he or she will be the one upon whom the next miracle will be wrought. The pilgrims who come are not confined to the Catholic faith. All denominations are represented there at various times.

The chapel is opened at five o'clock in the morning, and

from that time until nine o'clock at night there is always one or more persons kneeling upon the marble slab above the Bishop's dust.

One of the most marvelous cures witnessed by a father was laid before the court of inquiry at Rome. It was the case of a little boy who was ruptured. When, with his mother, he passed the priest, as he was being taken to the chapel, the priest spoke and asked what was the matter with him that he looked so extremely ill. His mother told the father the circumstances. When the boy was taken home he was cured. He ran and played about as other children, and from that day had no further trouble. Written statements from the doctor who pronounced his illness a rupture and from the physician who examined him later, saying there was nothing the matter with him, were taken to Rome and laid before the court of inquiry.

It is said that consumption has been cured there and cancer healed. The blind have seen and the paralyzed have walked. The tomb of Bishop Neuman gives evidence of becoming in time as celebrated for its miraculous cures as the shrine of St. Anne de Beaupre in Canada.

—*St. Louis, Globe Democrat.*

Note 5.

A System of Deception.

A case recently came to my knowledge, of a young lad, a son of Christian Science parents, who fell and hurt his forehead, producing a bruise, which became swollen to the size of half a hen's egg. His mother said to him: "my son, there is nothing the matter, you need pay no attention to it, there is absolutely nothing the matter." She washed the blood from the forehead, and the boy was soon out again playing with his companions. One of the neighbors, coming along, said to him: "why, Harry, what is the matter, you have a dreadful bruise." He replied, "there is nothing the matter, at all." But it was plainly evident, that something *was* the matter. The boy was being taught to delude himself. Now if this deception is taught and practiced in such things—may it not extend to others? If matter is "nothing" in such things as visible and bloody bruises, is matter anything, that one should hesitate to take, in the form of money or pocketbooks or anything that lies handy?

Note 6.

The Christian Science Theory Breaks at the Very Point Where Its Failure is Most Easily Demonstrated.

Mrs. Eddy says (page 392), "Have no fears that matter can ache, swell and be inflamed, from a law of any kind, when it is self-evident that matter can have no pain or inflammation. Your body would suffer no more from tension or wounds than the trunk of a tree which you gash, or the electric wire which you stretch, were it not for mortal mind." Yet Christian Scientists go to dentists to have their teeth—which are "illusions of the mortal mind" filled, with other "illusions of the mortal mind" or else to have the illusion extracted. Even Mrs. Eddy confesses (page 100) that in case a "false belief," called by ordinary people—a bone, becomes broken or dislocated, "it is better to refer such cases to a surgeon." Thus, it is in cases most capable of accurate observation, where the absurdity of the Christian Science theory becomes so evident that it is even by Mrs. Eddy a confessed failure.

As an illustration of the stupidity of Christian Science, an oculist gives a case in point. A convert to the "ism" who had trouble with one of her eyes, was treated by a healer, without success. In spite of all her efforts to make believe that "nothing was the matter," the eye continued to grow worse, until in desperation the woman went to consult an oculist. He discovered a very fine splinter, and removed it, and gave immediate relief. Here was a case where no amount of mental therapeutics of any sort could avail.

Note 7.

What Can Be Done?

In nearly every community in which Christian Science has made any progress, there are cases where the ignorance of the Christian Science practitioners, as to the nature and causes of disease, and their refusal to coöperate with physicians, have undoubtedly led to the premature death of patients. This is a sort of malpractice which is criminal. But Christian Scientists retort that when physicians are parties to the premature death of patients, nothing is said. And the fact that cases, which even skillful physicians have "given up," have been cured by the various methods of mental treatment, makes the plea plausible, and helps to prevent any steps being taken to protect the public.

But what can be done? Some urge that the state authorities should prevent any mental or metaphysical healer from taking charge of a case until the opinion of some competent physician has been obtained certifying that the case is a proper one for mental treatment. But here the "odium medicum" comes in, and there is no meeting ground. As long as the Christian Scientist bases his theory of healing on the non-existence of matter, and seeks to make people believe that he has a monopoly of the divine method of healing in order to bolster up his religion, of course no reputable physician could coöperate. The only solution that I can see, is for physicians generally (as some are doing) to study psychology and to recognize that psychic forces are far more potent than any others, in the treatment of certain diseases, when the public will cease to be fooled, and there will be no more need for Christian Scientists—nor Faith Curists " et id omne genus."

Note 8.

The Most Devoted Adherents.

ᴀt is often asked in surprise, how those who have lost members of their families by such diseases as diptheria, scarlet or typhoid fever, under Christian Science treatment, where lives have been sacrificed by the credulity of parents and the ignorance of Christian Science healers, it is asked how such people can have anything more to do with the fad? Yet it is just these people who are often the most devoted adherents to the cult. They cling to it with desperation, for the simple reason that if they ever allowed themselves to doubt it, their consciences would accuse them of being parties to the untimely death of those they loved.

www.ingramcontent.com/pod-product-compliance
Lightning Source LLC
Chambersburg PA
CBHW020234090426
42735CB00010B/1684